Janice VanCleave's
CRAZY, KOOKY, AND QUIRKY
Science Experiments

Janice VanCleave's
Crazy, Kooky, and Quirky
EARTH SCIENCE
EXPERIMENTS

Illustrations by
Jim Carroll

rosen publishing's
rosen central®

New York

This edition published in 2019 by
The Rosen Publishing Group, Inc.
29 East 21st Street
New York, NY 10010

Library of Congress Cataloging-in-Publication Data

Names: VanCleave, Janice Pratt, author.
Title: Janice VanCleave's crazy, kooky, and quirky earth science experiments / Janice VanCleave.
Description: New York : Rosen Central, 2019 | Series: Janice VanCleave's crazy, kooky, and quirky science experiments | Audience: Grades 5–8. | Includes bibliographical references and index.
Identifiers: LCCN 2017059630| ISBN 9781508180982 (library bound) | ISBN 9781508181033 (pbk.)
Subjects: LCSH: Earth sciences—Experiments—Juvenile literature. | Science projects—Juvenile literature.
Classification: LCC QE29 .V35945 2019 | DDC 550.78—dc23
LC record available at https://lccn.loc.gov/2017059630

Manufactured in the United States of America

Experiments first published in *Janice VanCleave's 203 Icy, Freezing, Frosty, Cool, and Wild Experiments* by John Wiley & Sons, Inc. copyright © 1999 Janice VanCleave

CONTENTS

INTRODUCTION

Earth science is the study of Earth. Geology is one main area of earth science that deals with the study of our physical planet. But oceanography, meteorology, and astronomy are also areas of earth science.

The people who decide to work in the field of earth science have a variety of career paths to choose from. Some work in laboratories. Others work outdoors and study soil, fossils, volcanos, and earthquakes. All of these people have something in common: they are constantly asking questions to learn even more about our planet.

This book is a collection of science experiments about earth science. Can you grow a crystal? How does frost form? How can global warming raise sea levels? You will find the answers to these and many other questions by doing the experiments in this book.

HOW TO USE THIS BOOK

You will be rewarded with successful experiments if you read each experiment carefully, follow the steps in order, and do not substitute materials. The following sections are included for all the experiments.

» **PURPOSE:** *The basic goals for the experiment.*

» **MATERIALS:** *A list of supplies you will need.* You will experience less frustration and more fun if you gather all the necessary materials for the experiments before you begin. You lose your train of thought when you have to stop and search for supplies.

» **PROCEDURE:** *Step-by-step instructions on how to perform the experiment.* Follow each step very carefully, never skip steps, and do not add your own. Safety is of the utmost importance, and by reading the experiment before starting and then following the instructions exactly, you can feel confident that no unexpected results will occur. Ask an adult to help you when you are working with anything sharp or hot. If adult supervision is required, it will be noted in the experiment.

» **RESULTS:** *An explanation stating exactly what is expected to happen.* This is an immediate learning tool. If the expected results are achieved, you will know that you did the experiment correctly. If your results are not the same as described in the experiment, carefully read the instructions and start over from the first step.

» **WHY?** *An explanation of why the results were achieved.*

INTRODUCTION

THE SCIENTIFIC METHOD

Scientists identify a problem or observe an event. Then they seek solutions or explanations through research and experimentation. By doing the experiments in this book, you will learn to follow experimental steps and make observations. You will also learn many scientific principles that have to do with earth science.

In the process, the things you see or learn may lead you to new questions. For example, perhaps you have completed the experiment that demonstrates how igneous rock forms. Now you wonder whether air temperature has an effect on its formation. That's great! All scientists are curious and ask new questions about what they learn. When you design a new experiment, it is a good idea to follow the scientific method.

1. Ask a question.

2. Do some research about your question. What do you already know?

3. Come up with a hypothesis, or a possible answer to your question.

4. Design an experiment to test your hypothesis. Make sure the experiment is repeatable.

5. Collect the data and make observations.

6. Analyze your results.

7. Reach a conclusion. Did your results support your hypothesis?

Many times the experiment leads to more questions and a new experiment.

Always remember that when devising your own science experiment, have a knowledgeable adult review it with you before trying it out. Ask him or her to supervise it as well.

FROSTY

PURPOSE To demonstrate how frost forms.

MATERIALS

7-ounce (210 mL) plastic
  drinking glass
ice
tap water

paper towel
4 tablespoons (60 mL) rock salt
  (used to make homemade ice cream)
timer

PROCEDURE

1. Fill the glass three-fourths full with ice, then cover the ice with water.

2. Dry the outside of the glass with the paper towel. Then sprinkle the salt over the ice.

3. Gently shake the glass back and forth four or five times to mix the ice, water, and salt.

4. Scratch the layer that forms on the outside of the glass with your fingernail every 15 seconds for 2 minutes. Observe the changes in the layer.

RESULTS A very thin layer of soft white ice forms on the outside of the glass, usually during the first 15 to 30 seconds. The frosty layer of ice is thicker after 2 minutes.

WHY? Frost is a light deposit of small, thin crystals of ice that form on cold objects when water vapor changes directly into a solid. Frost occurs when a layer of moist air comes in contact with a surface having a temperature below freezing (32°F, 0°C). Salt lowers the temperature of the icy water below freezing, which cools the glass to a below-freezing temperature. The change from a gas directly to a solid without forming a liquid is called sublimation.

STORMY

PURPOSE To model the eye of a hurricane.

MATERIALS

2-quart (2 liter) plastic bowl
tap water
scissors
string
ruler (the kind that has been
   punched for a three-ring binder)

paper clip
masking tape
black pepper
long-handled wooden spoon

PROCEDURE

1. Fill the plastic bowl three-fourths full with water.

2. Cut the string so that it is 1 inch (2.5 cm) longer than the height of the plastic bowl. Tie one end of the string to the paper clip.

3. Thread about 1 inch (2.5 cm) of the free end of the string through the hole in the center of the ruler. Tape the end to the ruler.

4. Sprinkle pepper over the surface of the water in the bowl. Stir the water with the spoon in a counterclockwise direction a few times.

5. While the water is swirling, quickly suspend the paper clip in the center of the water. Try to drop the paper clip directly in the center of the spiral made by the swirling specks.

RESULTS As long as the paper clip remains in the exact center of the swirling water, it moves slightly or not at all.

WHY? The swirling water in the experiment represents a hurricane. A hurricane is a large tropical storm with winds of 74 miles per hour (118 kmh) or more that rotate around a relatively calm center. The center of the swirling water in this experiment simulates the calm area in the center of a hurricane, called the eye of a hurricane. The eye is a long, vertical tube of relatively motionless air in the middle of the storm.

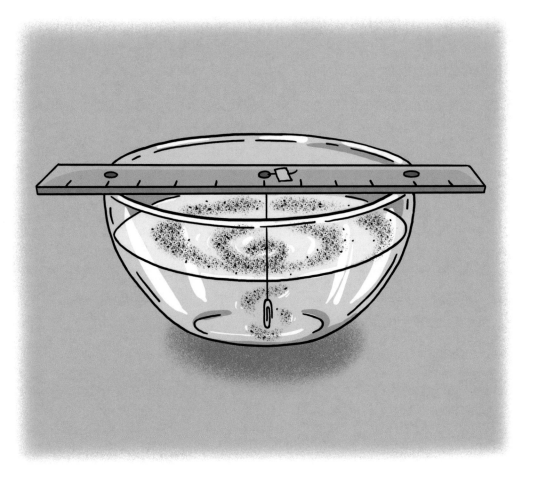

RAINDROPS

PURPOSE To measure the size of water drops.

MATERIALS

1 cup (250 mL) flour
strainer
cake pan
spray bottle filled with tap water
large serving spoon

large bowl
sheet of dark-colored
 construction paper
pencil
metric ruler
magnifying lens

PROCEDURE

1. Sift the flour through the strainer into the cake pan. Discard any flour particles that do not fall through the strainer.
Set the pan on a table, and spray a mist of water from the spray bottle so that it falls on the surface of the flour.

2. Use the spoon to scoop 1 to 2 spoonfuls of flour from the pan into the strainer. Scoop the drops of water along with the flour.
Hold the strainer over the bowl and gently shake it back and forth so that the flour falls through the holes in the strainer and into the bowl. Shake the strainer until all loose flour falls into the bowl and balls of flour remain in the strainer.

3. Pour the flour balls from the strainer onto the paper.

4. Repeat steps 3 to 5 until all the flour in the pan has been sifted and all the flour balls collected.

5. Measure the size of several of the flour balls, one ball at a time, by using the tip of the pencil to move each ball next to the ruler. Using the magnifying lens to see, move the ruler so that the left side of the ball is in line with a measuring mark.

RESULTS A variety of different-size flour balls are formed.

WHY? The water from the spray mist falls like raindrops on the surface of the flour. When the drops hit the flour's surface, fine particles of flour coat the outside of the drop. The flour coating on each water drop only slightly increases the size of the drop of water. Thus, the flour ball can be measured to determine the approximate size of the drop inside it.

WET AND DRY

PURPOSE To make a thread hygrometer.

MATERIALS

scissors
ruler
1-by-2-inch (2.5-by-5 cm)
   rectangle of poster board
one-hole paper punch
hammer
two size 3 finishing nails
   (Any small-head nail about
   1 inch, 2.5 cm, long will work.)

2-by-4-by-12-inch (5-by-10-by-30 cm)
   board (Size of board is not critical.)
silk thread (available where embroidery
   floss is sold)
pen
protractor

PROCEDURE

1. Make a pointer by cutting a triangle with a 1-inch (2.5 cm) base and a 2-inch (5 cm) height from the poster board. Use the paper punch to cut two holes along the height of the triangle. Make one hole near the base and the other near the tip.

2. Hammer a nail into the board about 1 inch (2.5 cm) in from one corner.

3. Hang the pointer on the nail by the hole near the base.

4. Tie one end of the silk thread to the other hole in the pointer. Hold the free end of the thread against the board so that the base of the pointer is parallel to the edge of the board. Hammer the second nail into the board near the end of the strand, and tie the strand to the nail.

5. Use the pen and protractor to make six to eight marks at five intervals in an arc around the tip of the pointer.

6. Observe the position of the pointer on humid and dry days.

RESULTS The pointer moves up on dry days and down on wet days.

WHY? You have made a thread hygrometer, an instrument that can be used to indicate changes in humidity (the amount of water in the air). The thread expands when the humidity increases and contracts when the humidity decreases. The expansion and contraction of the thread lowers and raises the pointer.

COILED

PURPOSE To make a paper hygrometer.

MATERIALS

1-by-10-inch (2.5-by-25 cm)
   strip of newspaper
4-by-12-inch (10-by-30 cm)
   strip of aluminum foil
transparent tape
scissors

short pencil about 6 inches (15 cm) long
1-quart (1 liter) jar with lid
thread spool
pen
writing paper

PROCEDURE

1. Lay the newspaper strip in the center of the foil. Tape the paper to the foil with a single layer of tape along all edges of the paper.

2. Trim the foil edges, leaving about ¼ inch (0.63 cm) of foil around the paper on all sides.

3. Tape one end of the strip to the pencil below the eraser cap. Wind the strip snugly around the pencil so that the foil is on the outside.

4. Stand the writing end of the pencil in the hole in the thread spool, then set the spool inside the open jar.

5. Observe the strip periodically for several days, noting how tightly it is coiled around the pencil on dry and humid days.

RESULTS The paper is more loosely coiled on humid days than on dry days.

WHY? The newspaper is hygroscopic, which means it absorbs water from the air. As the pores in the paper fill with water, the paper expands and pushes against the foil, which is not hygroscopic. The force of the expanding paper causes the coil to unwind. The paper coil acts as a hygrometer. The higher the humidity, the more water available for the coil to absorb and the more the coil expands.

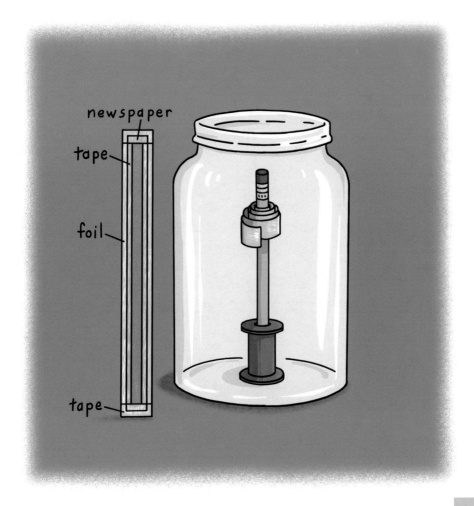

CHANGED

PURPOSE To demonstrate how rusting weathers a rock.

MATERIALS cup
tap water
rubber gloves
lemon-size steel wool pad without soap
(available at stores that carry painting supplies)
saucer
clear plastic drinking glass

PROCEDURE

CAUTION: *Steel wool can splinter. Wear rubber gloves when handling steel wool.*

1. Fill the cup halfway with water.

2. Put on the rubber gloves, then dip the steel wool pad into the cup of water. Hold the steel wool above the cup and allow the excess water to drain into the cup.

3. Place the moistened steel wool on the saucer, then invert the drinking glass and stand it in the saucer so that it covers all of the steel wool.

4. Place the saucer where it will not be disturbed for five days. Each day, put on the rubber gloves, pick up the steel wool, and rub the wool between your fingers. Observe what happens to the steel wool.

RESULTS Each day, more of the steel wool turns reddish brown and crumbles when touched.

WHY? In the presence of water, oxygen in the air combines with the iron in the steel wool pad to form iron oxide, commonly called rust. Rusting (the process by which a substance rusts) is a type of chemical weathering (the breakdown of rocks by changes in their chemical composition). The rust weakens the structure of the steel wool, like the structure of rocks, causing it to fall apart when touched.

MELTDOWN

PURPOSE To model how rocks melt.

MATERIALS

cup of warm tap water
spoon
timer
toothpick

½-by-½-inch (1.25-by-1.25 cm)
    square of milk chocolate candy
saucer

PROCEDURE

1. Fill the cup with warm tap water.

2. Place the spoon in the cup of water.

3. After about 30 seconds, remove the spoon from the water, place the chocolate in the spoon, and set the spoon on the saucer.

4. Use the toothpick to move the chocolate around in the spoon.

RESULTS The chocolate melts.

WHY? Melting is the change of a solid to a liquid as a result of an increase in energy, such as heat. Chocolate is solid at room temperature, but like all solids, it melts when heated. The temperature at which a solid melts is called its melting point. The change in the chocolate from a solid to a liquid due to an increase in its temperature is similar to the change of solid rock to magma (liquid rock beneath Earth's surface). Rocks have a much higher melting point than the chocolate. The tremendous heat at depths of about 25 to 37.5 miles (40 to 60 km) below Earth's surface is great enough to melt rock.

EASY FLOW

PURPOSE To model how pressure affects the rock in the asthenosphere.

MATERIALS

1-cup (250 mL) measuring cup
tap water
9-oz (270 mL) plastic drinking glass
1-tablespoon (15 mL) measuring spoon

10 tablespoons (150 mL)
   cornstarch
spoon
bowl

PROCEDURE

1. Prepare the simulated "putty rock" (the layer below the crust): Pour ¼ cup (63 mL) of water into the plastic glass. Add 1 level tablespoon (15 mL) of cornstarch and stir well. Continue adding cornstarch, 1 tablespoon (15 mL) at a time. Stir well after each addition. The mixture should be thick enough that it is very hard to stir. Add a few drops of water if all of the starch will not dissolve, or add a little starch if the mixture looks thin.

2. Set the bowl on a table. Hold the glass containing the putty rock in one hand, and tilt the glass slightly so that about half of the material flows slowly into the bowl. Observe how the material flows.

3. Use the spoon to scrape the rest of the material out of the glass and into the bowl. Observe how the material behaves when forced to move.

RESULTS The material flows easily out of the glass when not forced, but cracks and breaks if pressure is applied.

WHY? Earth's crust (outer layer) and the upper portion of its mantle (the layer below the crust) make up a layer called the lithosphere. Below the lithosphere is a portion of the mantle called the asthenosphere. In this zone, the rock making up the mantle behaves like both a liquid and a solid. Rock in the asthenosphere is thought to behave like the simulated putty rock prepared in the experiment—it flows easily if moved slowly, but thickens and breaks if pressure is applied. This ability of a solid material to flow is called plasticity.

LAYERING

PURPOSE To simulate how deposited sediments form layers in the bottom of a lake.

MATERIALS ½ cup (125 mL) each of 3 different colors
of aquarium gravel
3 bowls
1 ½ cups (375 mL) soil or sand
spoon
2-quart (2 liter) rectangular glass baking dish
tap water
timer

PROCEDURE

Pour one cup of gravel into each of the three bowls.

1. Add ½ cup (125 mL) of soil or sand to each bowl of gravel. Use the spoon to mix the gravel and soil thoroughly.

2. Fill the baking dish half full with water.

3. Use your hand to slowly sprinkle the gravel-and-soil mixture from one of the bowls into the water. Wait 10 minutes and observe the appearance of the materials in the dish.

4. Sprinkle the gravel-and-soil mixture from one of the remaining bowls into the water. Again wait 10 minutes and observe the appearance of the materials.

5. Add the remaining gravel-and-soil mixture. After 10 minutes, observe the contents of the dish.

RESULTS The three different-colored mixtures form separate layers in the dish.

WHY? Regolith is the loose, uncemented rock particles, including soil, that cover Earth. Sediments are regoliths that have been transported by agents of erosion (substances that cause erosion: wind, water, and ice) and deposited in another place. The sediments in this experiment (gravel and soil) sank through the water to form layers. Because the mixtures of gravel and soil were added at 10-minute intervals, the bottom layer is relatively older and the top layer is relatively younger than the other layers. Layers of rock are believed to form in a similar manner, and like the gravel-and-soil mixture, each rock layer is laid down on top of the one beneath it. This is how scientists can tell the relative age of each layer.

BOBBER

PURPOSE To determine if surface water moves with each wave.

MATERIALS

large, rectangular glass baking dish
tap water
scissors
ruler

drinking straw
timer
unsharpened pencil

PROCEDURE

1. Fill the baking dish three-fourths full with water.

2. Cut about 1 inch (2.5 cm) from one end of the straw.

3. Place the small piece of straw in the center of the water in the dish. Wait about 30 seconds to allow the water to become calm.

4. With the unsharpened end of the pencil, tap the surface of the water at one end of the dish. Observe the straw and the surface of the water.

RESULTS Waves start where the water is touched by the pencil, move to the opposite end of the dish, and return again. This back-and-forth movement of the waves may happen several times. While the waves are moving back and forth across the surface, the straw is moving up and down.

WHY? A water wave is a disturbance on the surface of water that repeats itself. In waves, energy is transferred from one water molecule to the next. As the energy of a water wave moves forward, the water moves up and down, but there is only a slight horizontal movement of the water molecules. Thus, objects floating on the water's surface may move horizontally slightly, but mostly they bob up and down as waves pass through the water.

RISING

PURPOSE To show how global warming could raise sea level.

MATERIALS

5-ounce (150 mL) paper cup
tap water
cereal bowl

ruler
lemon-size piece of modeling clay
timer

PROCEDURE

1. Fill the paper cup with water and place it in a freezer overnight.

2. Tear the paper cup away from the ice, then stand the ice in the bowl.

3. Mold the clay into an island shape with a high center and a shoreline that's about ½ inch (1.25 cm) thick. Place the clay island in the bowl and press it against the bottom of the bowl.

4. Add about ¼ inch (0.63 cm) of water to the bowl.

5. Observe the water level on the shore of your island every 20 minutes or so until the ice block melts. This will take about 2 hours.

RESULTS The level of the water rises and may cover part of the clay's shoreline.

WHY? As the ice warms, it changes from a solid to a liquid. This liquid water spreads out and mixes with the water in the bowl, causing the volume of the water to increase and the water level to rise. If global warming (an increase in the average temperature of Earth) is great enough, polar ice (large masses of ice in the Arctic and Antarctic regions)

28

will melt, raising sea level and flooding coastlines. Scientists think the burning of fossil fuels (energy sources, including coal and natural gas, made of buried remains of decayed plants and animals that lived hundreds of millions of years ago), which increases the amount of carbon dioxide in the atmosphere, is causing the atmosphere to warm. It is extremely likely, although not certain, that global warming is the result of mankind's influence on the climate and not a natural long-term geologic pattern.

TABLETOP

PURPOSE To model an Antarctic iceberg.

MATERIALS

12-by-18-inch (30-by-45 cm) piece of
  heavy-duty aluminum foil
tap water
saucer

2-quart (2 liter) transparent bowl
1 tablespoon (15 mL) table salt
spoon

PROCEDURE

1. Make a shallow box out of foil:

   - Fold the foil in half three times to make a 4 ½-by-6-inch (11.25-by-15 cm) rectangle.

   - Fold up about 1 inch (2.5 cm) of each edge of the rectangle to make the sides of the box.

   - Fold the foil to one side at each corner so that it is snug against the sides of the box.

2. Fill the foil box with water.

3. Set the water-filled box on the saucer and put the saucer in the freezer for 3 hours or until the water in the box is completely frozen.

4. Fill the bowl three-fourths full with water, then add the table salt and stir.

5. Peel the foil box away from the ice.

6. Place the ice in the bowl. Observe the amount of ice above and below the surface of the water.

RESULTS More of the ice is below the water's surface than above it.

WHY? When water freezes, it expands. The density of icebergs is slightly less than the density of salty ocean water. As a result, the iceberg floats, with about six-sevenths of the iceberg below the ocean surface. Icebergs in the Antarctic are tabular (shaped like a tabletop) like the ice in this experiment. Antarctic icebergs are more abundant and much larger than those in the Arctic. It is not unusual for Antarctic icebergs to be several miles long while Arctic icebergs generally have lengths of about 600 feet (180 m).

PATTERNS

PURPOSE To demonstrate how atoms and molecules arrange themselves in minerals.

MATERIALS large, shallow baking pan
tap water
1 teaspoon (5 mL) dishwashing liquid
spoon
drinking straw

PROCEDURE

1. Fill the pan half full with water, then add the dishwashing liquid. Gently stir.

2. Place one end of the straw beneath the surface of the water. Slowly and gently blow through the straw to make a cluster of 5 to 15 bubbles. *CAUTION: Only exhale through the straw. Do not inhale.*

3. Move the straw to a different location and blow a single bubble.

4. With the straw, move the bubble so that it touches the bubble cluster.

RESULTS The single bubble attaches to the bubble cluster.

WHY? The bubbles represent the chemical particles of a mineral. Chemical particles are the atoms or molecules that make up minerals and matter. Minerals are substances found in the ground that do not come from living things, and have a definite chemical composition and a regular crystal form. The addition of the bubble to the bubble cluster represents the growth of a mineral crystal. Chemical particles, like the bubbles, can move around in a liquid. Just as a single bubble moves to a place where it fits in the bubble cluster, chemical particles dissolved in a liquid move to just the right spot in order to fit with other particles. Once a chemical particle like the bubble moves into the right place, it is held there by the attraction it has to the other chemical particles.

OVERFLOW

PURPOSE To make an instrument to determine specific gravity.

MATERIALS

scissors
ruler
2-liter soda bottle
one-hole paper punch
flexible drinking straw

2-cup (500 mL) measuring cup
pitcher
tap water
adult helper

PROCEDURE

1. Ask an adult to cut about 4 inches (10 cm) off the top of the soda bottle.

2. Use the paper punch to make a hole about 1 inch (2.5 cm) from the rim of the bottle.

3. Insert about ½ inch (1.25 cm) of the flexible end of the straw in the hole. Bend the straw so that it forms a 90° angle. Place the measuring cup under the free end of the straw.

4. Use the pitcher to pour water into the bottle until it is just above the straw. Water will flow through the straw and into the cup.

5. When the water stops flowing into the cup, empty the cup, then set the cup in place under the straw. The water-filled bottle and the empty cup are your specific gravity instrument.

6. Push your fingers into the water in the bottle and note the amount of water that flows into the cup.
NOTE: Keep the instrument for the next experiment.

RESULTS The amount of water in the cup will depend on the size of your fingers.

WHY? Specific gravity is the ratio of the mass of a substance, such as your finger, compared to the mass of an equal volume of water. Your specific gravity instrument does not measure mass, but it does allow you to determine the volume of water equal to the volume of an object being measured. This is done by collecting the water displaced (pushed out of place) by an object placed in the instrument.

Heavy

PURPOSE To calculate the specific gravity of a mineral.

MATERIALS 24-inch (60 cm) piece of string

fist-size sample of quartz, or any mineral of
comparable size

food scale that measures in grams

paper

pencil

specific gravity instrument from the experiment "Overflow"

PROCEDURE

1. Tie the string around the mineral, then place the mineral on the scale to determine as accurately as possible its mass in grams (g). Record the mass.
Repeat steps 5 and 6 in "Overflow."

2. Holding the mineral by the string, slowly lower it into the bottle. Do not let the water spill over the rim of the bottle.

3. When the water stops flowing into the measuring cup, record the amount of water in the cup in milliliters (mL). Use the following example to determine the specific gravity of your mineral specimen:

Example: A mineral with a mass of 150 g displaces 60 mL of water.

- Specific gravity (SG) = mass of mineral divided by mass of water displaced by mineral

- Mass of mineral = 150 g

- Volume of displaced water = 60 mL

- 1 mL water has a mass of 1 g, so the mass of displaced water = 60 g

SG = 150 g ÷ 60 g = 2.5

RESULTS The specific gravity of the mineral in the example is 2.5.

WHY? Mass is measured with SI units of grams. It has been determined that 1 pound of weight, a measure of the gravitational force between two objects, on Earth is equal to a mass of 454 g. Scales indicating gram units have been designed to show the mass of a given weight. To calculate SG, divide the mass of the mineral by the mass of the water displaced by the mineral. The answer tells you how many times more massive or heavier the mineral is than water. The mineral in the example is 2.5 times as heavy as water. Most minerals have a specific gravity greater than 1, meaning that they are heavier than water. Every substance has a certain SG, thus the SG of any substance can be a clue to its identity.

SCRATCH

PURPOSE To use a method for determining the hardness of a mineral.

MATERIALS sharpened No. 2 pencil

PROCEDURE

1. Hold the pencil against a table with one hand.

2. With your other hand, scratch the pencil lead with a fingernail.

3. Observe the ease or difficulty of making a scratch in the pencil lead.

RESULTS Your fingernail easily cuts a groove in the pencil lead.

WHY? The hardness of a mineral is its resistance to being scratched. Frederick Mohs (1773–1839), a German chemist, arranged ten common minerals into a hardness scale. He gave the softest mineral, talc, the number 1, and the hardest mineral, diamond, the number 10. The hardness value of a mineral is determined by how easily it can be scratched when rubbed by another mineral or material of known hardness. The rule is that a mineral can scratch any mineral or material with a lower hardness number. Your fingernail has a hardness of about 2 ½. Since your nail can scratch the graphite-and-clay mixture that makes up the pencil lead, the hardness of the graphite-and-clay mixture must be less than 2 ½.

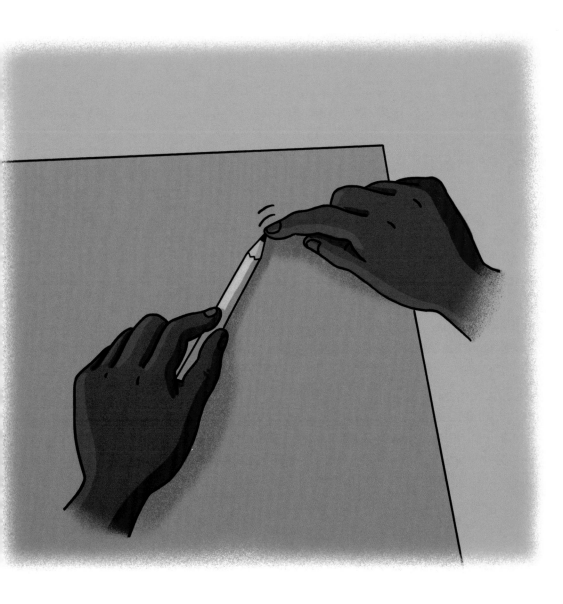

Scratch

POWDERED

PURPOSE To use a method for determining the streak of a mineral.

MATERIALS piece of gypsum

sheet of very fine sandpaper

NOTE: White school chalk is not a mineral but can be substituted for gypsum in this experiment if gypsum is not available.

PROCEDURE

1. Rub the gypsum back and forth across the sandpaper three or four times.

2. Observe the color of the streak made by the gypsum on the sandpaper.

RESULTS The color of the streak is white.

WHY? The sandpaper is harder than the gypsum. Rubbing the gypsum across the rough, hard surface of the sandpaper removes fine particles of gypsum. These particles produce the white streak on the paper. Thus, the streak of a mineral is the color of the powder left when the mineral is rubbed against a rough surface that is harder than the mineral. The color and the streak of gypsum are the same, but this is not true for all minerals. Since a mineral's streak can be different from its color, its streak is used for identification.

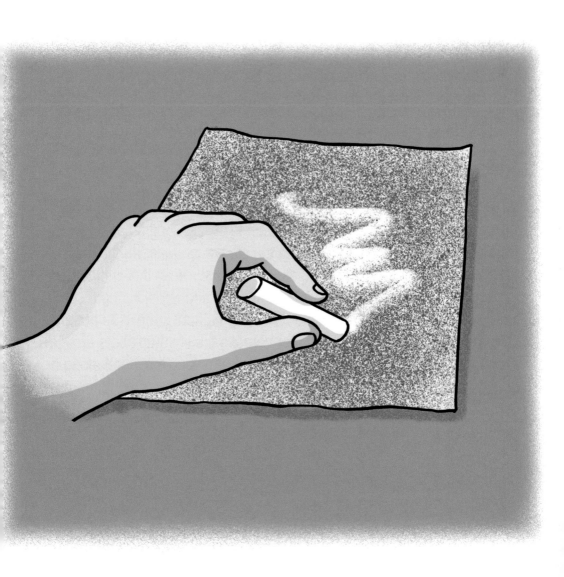

Powdered

Smooth

PURPOSE To model cleavage of a mineral.

MATERIALS sheet of newspaper

PROCEDURE

1. Hold the sheet of newspaper with both hands so that your thumbs meet in the center along the top of the sheet.

2. Tear the sheet of paper in half from top to bottom.

RESULTS The paper tears in a relatively straight line down the page.

WHY? One of the ways a mineral breaks is by cleavage. Cleavage is the property of a mineral that allows it to break along a flat smooth area called a cleavage pane. Along the cleavage plane, the bonds between atoms are relatively weak. (Bonds are forces that link atoms, groups of atoms, or molecules together.) The fibers making up a sheet of newspaper are generally lined up from the paper's top to its bottom. Tearing the paper from top to bottom breaks the lined-up fibers apart in a relatively straight, smooth line, much like breaking a mineral along a cleavage plane breaks the mineral apart, exposing two smooth edges.

ZIGZAG

PURPOSE To model fracturing of a mineral.

MATERIALS sheet of newspaper

PROCEDURE

1. Hold the sheet of newspaper with both hands so that your thumbs meet in the center along one side of the sheet.

2. Tear the sheet of paper in half from one side to the other.

RESULTS The paper tears in a zigzag line.

WHY? Fracturing is the breaking of a mineral across a cleavage plane, exposing uneven or jagged edges. Since the fibers of a newspaper generally line up from top to bottom on the sheet, tearing the sheet from side to side cuts across these lines of fibers. The result is a jagged tear, much like what happens when a mineral is broken across its cleavage plane. Paper is easily torn along or across its cleavage plane. But it is more difficult to fracture a mineral than to cleave it. This is because the bonds are stronger between atoms that are not in line with the cleavage plate.

STRETCHED

PURPOSE To model the effect of tension on rock.

MATERIALS 4 golf-ball size pieces of modeling clay, each a different color

PROCEDURE

1. Shape each ball of clay into a piece about 2 inches (5 cm) wide, 4 inches (10 cm) long, and ¼ inch (0.63 cm) thick. Stack the pieces to make one big piece with four layers.

2. Hold the ends of the clay and slowly pull outward. Observe the shape of the clay as it is being pulled.

RESULTS The layers of clay stretch, making the center section thinner.

WHY? The different layers of clay represent strata (layers of one kind of rock material) of rock in the ground. Pulling on the clay layers models tension, a type of stress (a deforming force) by which rocks are stretched or pulled apart. This occurs when the strata are pulled apart during an earthquake (a sudden movement or shaking of Earth's crust).

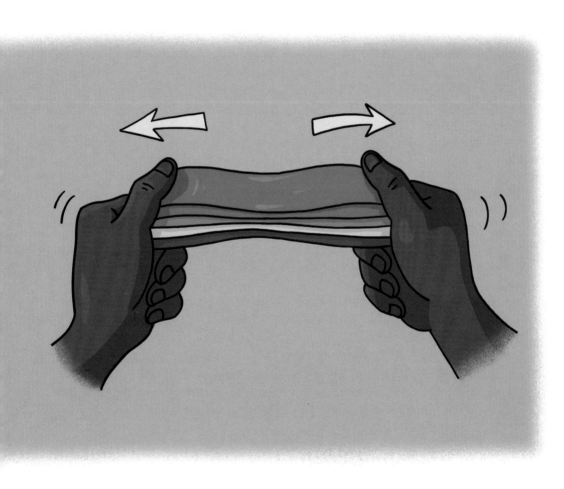

Stretched

HOT ROCKS

PURPOSE To model how igneous rock is formed.

MATERIALS

deep bowl
strainer large enough to fit across the bowl
4 sheets of construction paper—2 white,
   1 blue, 1 red
food blender (to be used only by an adult)
4 cups (1 liter) tap water

2 teaspoons (30 mL) white
   school glue
timer
10 to 12 sheets of newspaper
adult helper

PROCEDURE

1. Set the strainer across the mouth of the bowl.

2. Tear one sheet of white and blue construction paper into small pieces.

3. Drop the paper pieces into the blender, then add half of the water and glue to the blender.

4. Ask an adult to turn on the blender and thoroughly mix the paper and water. A thick paper mulch will be produced.

5. Pour the paper mulch into the strainer over the bowl, and let it sit undisturbed for about 20 minutes.

6. After 20 minutes, fold 5 to 6 of the newspaper sheets in half and lay them on the table. Pick up the wet paper mulch with your hand and place it on top of the newspaper.

7. Allow the paper mulch to dry and solidify. This may take 2 to 3 days.

8. Repeat steps 1 through 7, using the remaining materials.

NOTE: Keep the dry mulches for the next experiment.

RESULTS The two colors of mulch, blue and pink, become lumpy solids.

WHY? The blending of different-colored paper pieces and water represents the melting of different rocks beneath the surface of Earth due to heat and pressure. This melted rock is called magma. When magma rises to the surface of Earth, it is then called lava. Magma and lava cool and solidify to form a type of rock called igneous rock. The drying of the paper mulches represents the cooling of magma or lava to form igneous rocks.

TRANSFORMED

PURPOSE To model the transformation of igneous rock into sedimentary rock.

MATERIALS 2 mock igneous rocks from the Experiment "Hot Rocks"
10 to 12 sheets of newspaper
white school glue

PROCEDURE

1. Break half of the pink rock into small pieces and lay the pieces in a thin layer on top of the newspapers.

2. Cover the top of the broken pieces of pink rock with glue, then press the pieces together with your hands.

3. Make a second layer, using pieces from half of the blue rock. Again, cover with glue and press the two layers together.

4. Add a third and fourth layer, alternating the pink and blue rocks.

5. Allow the material to dry. This may take 2 hours or more.

RESULTS A solid form with alternating layers of colored mock rock is made.

WHY? Igneous rock, like all rocks, can be transformed into sedimentary rock (rock formed by deposit of sediments). First, rocks are eroded (worn away), which means they weather, forming small particles that are moved by agents of erosion, including wind and rain. These particles are called sediment (represented by broken pieces of the mock rocks).

Newly deposited sediments don't fit together tightly, so the spaces fill up with water, which often contains minerals (represented by the glue). More layers of sediment are added (represented by other layers of mock rock and glue). The weight of the layers presses on underlying sediments, compacting them. Compaction squeezes the water out, leaving minerals that glue the sediments together. This process of rock layer formation is called cementation (represented by the drying of the glue).

SPACEY

PURPOSE To determine how soil texture affects the amount of air in soil.

MATERIALS

spoon
1 cup (250 mL) coarse soil
2-cup (500 mL) measuring cup with
    ounce measurements

tap water
paper
pencil
1 cup (250 mL) fine soil

PROCEDURE

1. Use the spoon to add 8 ounces (240 mL) of coarse soil to the larger measuring cup. Do not press against the surface of the soil as you gently add the soil to the cup.

2. Slowly add 8 ounces (240 mL) of water to the cup of soil. Record the combined volume of the soil and water.

3. Use the following example to calculate the volume of air in the soil: *total volume* (volume of soil by itself + volume of water by itself) = 16 ounces (480 mL). The *combined volume* (volume of soil and water in cup) = 12 ounces (360 mL). The air volume (*total volume – combined volume*) = 4 ounces (120 mL). So, there are 4 ounces (120 mL) of air in the coarse soil.

4. Repeat the procedure, using the fine soil. Compare the air volumes.

RESULTS The coarse soil has more air than the fine soil.

WHY? The particles of coarse soil are larger. All soil particles are irregular in shape, and as they stack together there is space between them, which fills with air. Larger soil particles have more space between them. When soil and water are mixed, the air between the soil particles is displaced by water. Thus, the larger or more coarse the soil particles, the more air the soil contains.

CRYSTALS

PURPOSE To grow crystals.

MATERIALS

¼ teaspoon (1.25 mL) dishwashing liquid
clear, transparent plastic folder
small paintbrush
1 tablespoon (15 mL) Epsom salts
clear drinking glass

1-tablespoon (15 mL)
 measuring spoon
tap water
spoon
paper and pencil

PROCEDURE

1. Pour the dishwashing liquid onto the center of the plastic folder. Use the paintbrush to evenly spread the dishwashing liquid over the surface of one side of the folder. Allow the dishwashing liquid to dry.

2. Place the Epsom salts in the glass, then add 3 tablespoons (45 mL) of warm water and stir until all of the salt dissolves.

3. Place 3 tablespoons (45 mL) of the Epsom salts solution on top of the dried detergent layer. Use the bowl of the spoon to spread the solution as evenly as possible over the folder's surface.

4. Observe and record the changes that occur. If the air is dry and warm, the results take about 30 minutes. A longer time is required in cold or humid air.

5. Look through the folder toward a light. Notice and record the shape of the crystals.

RESULTS Fans of long, clear, needle-shaped crystals form on the surface of the folder.

WHY? As the water evaporates, the Epsom salts molecules move closer together and bond, forming long, needle-shaped crystals. The shape of the Epsom salts crystals reflects the arrangement of the molecules in the solid. The molecules are arranged like building blocks that lock together, thus the shape of the molecules determines the shape of the resulting crystal. The dried dishwashing liquid provides a rough surface to which the crystals can stick.

GLOSSARY

BOND   A force that links atoms, groups of atoms, or molecules together.

CHEMICAL WEATHERING   The breakdown of rocks by changes in their chemical composition.

DISPLACE   To push out of place.

EARTHQUAKE   A sudden movement or shaking of Earth's crust.

ERODE   To wear away.

FOSSIL FUELS   Energy sources, including coal and natural gas, made of buried remains of decayed plants and animals that lived hundreds of millions of years ago.

GLOBAL WARMING   An increase in the average temperature of Earth.

HUMIDITY   The amount of water in the air.

HYGROMETER   An instrument that can be used to indicate changes in humidity.

LAVA   Magma that rises to the surface of Earth.

MAGMA   Liquid rock beneath Earth's surface.

MELTING   The change of a solid to a liquid as a result of an increase in energy, such as heat.

MINERAL A substance found in the ground that does not come from living things, and has a definite chemical composition and a regular crystal form.

PLASTICITY The ability of a solid material to flow.

POLAR ICE Large masses of ice in the Arctic and Antarctic regions.

RUSTING The process by which a substance rusts.

SPECIFIC GRAVITY The ratio of the mass of a substance compared to the mass of an equal volume of water.

SUBLIMATION The change from a gas directly to a solid without forming a liquid.

FOR MORE INFORMATION

Canadian Federation of Earth Sciences (CFES)
  Department of Earth Sciences
  FSS Hall
  Room 15025
  Ottawa, ON K1N 6N5
  Canada
  (902) 697-7425
  Website: http://www.cfes-fcst.ca
  The CFES is a federation of earth science member societies throughout
  Canada. Read about careers, get your earth science questions answered
  by an expert with the Ask a Geoscientist! tool, or use their Earth Links to
  find a multitude of resources about earth science.

National Aeronautics and Space Administration (NASA)
  Ames Earth Science Division
  NASA Headquarters
  300 E Street SW, Suite 5R30
  Washington, DC 20546
  (202) 358-0001
  Website: http://geo.arc.nasa.gov
  NASA is the premier organization for all things about space and planet
  Earth! Join the NASA Kids' Club, see photos of Earth from space, and
  learn more about earth science research.

National Center for Earth and Space Science Education (NCESSE)
  PO Box 2350
  Ellicott City, MD 21041-2350
  (301) 395-0770
  Website: http://ncesse.org
  The NCESSE creates and oversees national programs addressing

STEM education, with a focus on Earth and space. Check out their links to Family Science Night, contests, experiment programs, and other community events.

National Geographic Society
1145 17th Street NW
Washington, DC 20036
Museum (202) 857-7700
Website: http://www.nationalgeographic.com
The National Geographic Society has been inspiring people to care about the planet since 1888. It is one of the largest nonprofit scientific and educational institutions in the world. Read their *National Geographic Kids* magazine, enter the National Geographic Bee, or visit the museum.

National Science Foundation (NSF)
4201 Wilson Boulevard
Arlington, VA 22230
(703) 292-5111
Website: http://www.nsf.gov
The NSF is dedicated to science, engineering, and education. Learn how to be a Citizen Scientist, read about the latest scientific discoveries, and find out about the newest innovations in technology.

Society for Science and the Public
Student Science
1719 N Street NW
Washington, DC 20036
(800) 552-4412
Website: http://student.societyforscience.org

The Society for Science and the Public presents many science resources, such as science news for students, the latest updates on the Intel Science Talent Search and the Intel International Science and Engineering Fair, and information about cool jobs and doing science.

US Geological Survey (USGS)
12201 Sunrise Valley Drive
Reston, VA 20192
(888) 275-8747
Website: http://www.usgs.gov
The USGS collects, monitors, analyzes, and provides scientific data about natural resource conditions, issues, and problems on the earth. Check out their aerial and satellite images, use their many educational resources, or ask a librarian to help with your earth science questions.

FOR FURTHER READING

Ardley, Neil. *101 Great Science Experiments*. New York, NY: DK Ltd., 2014.

Buczynski, Sandy. *Designing a Winning Science Fair Project* (Information Explorer Junior). Ann Arbor, MI: Cherry Lake Publishing, 2014.

Dickmann, Nancy. *Exploring Planet Earth and the Moon* (Spectacular Space Science). New York, NY: Rosen Publishing's Rosen Central, 2016.

Gagne, Tammy. *Women in Earth and Space Exploration* (Women in STEM). Minneapolis, MN: Core Library, 2017.

Garbe, Suzanne. *Living Earth: Exploring Life on Earth with Science Projects* (Fact Finders: Discover Earth Science). North Mankato, MN: Capstone Press, 2016.

Harris, Tim, ed. *Earth Science* (Science Q&A). New York, NY: Cavendish Square, 2016.

Hyde, Natalie. *Earthquakes, Eruptions, and Other Events that Change Earth* (Earth Processes Close-Up). New York, NY: Crabtree Publishing Co., 2016.

Latta, Sara. *All About Earth: Exploring the Planet with Science Projects* (Fact Finders: Discover Earth Science). North Mankato, MN: Capstone Press, 2016.

Ruff Ruffman's *44 Favorite Science Activities* (Fetch! with Ruff Ruffman). Somerville, MA: Candlewick Press, 2015.

Shea, Therese. *Freaky Weather Stories* (Freaky True Science). New York, NY: Gareth Stevens Publishing, 2016.

Slingerland, Janet. *What Makes the Sky Blue?* (Everyday Earth Science). Mankato, MN: The Child's World, 2017.

Sneideman, Joshua. *Climate Change: Discover How It Impacts Spaceship Earth*. Whiter River Junction, VT: Nomad Press, 2015.

Sohn, Emily. *Experiments in Earth Science and Weather with Toys and Everyday Stuff* (First Facts: Fun Science). North Mankato, MN: Capstone Press, 2016.

Weakland, Mark. *Whoosh! Wilie E. Coyote Experiments with Flight and Gravity* (Wilie E. Coyote, Physical Science Genius). North Mankato, MN: Capstone Press, 2017.

INDEX